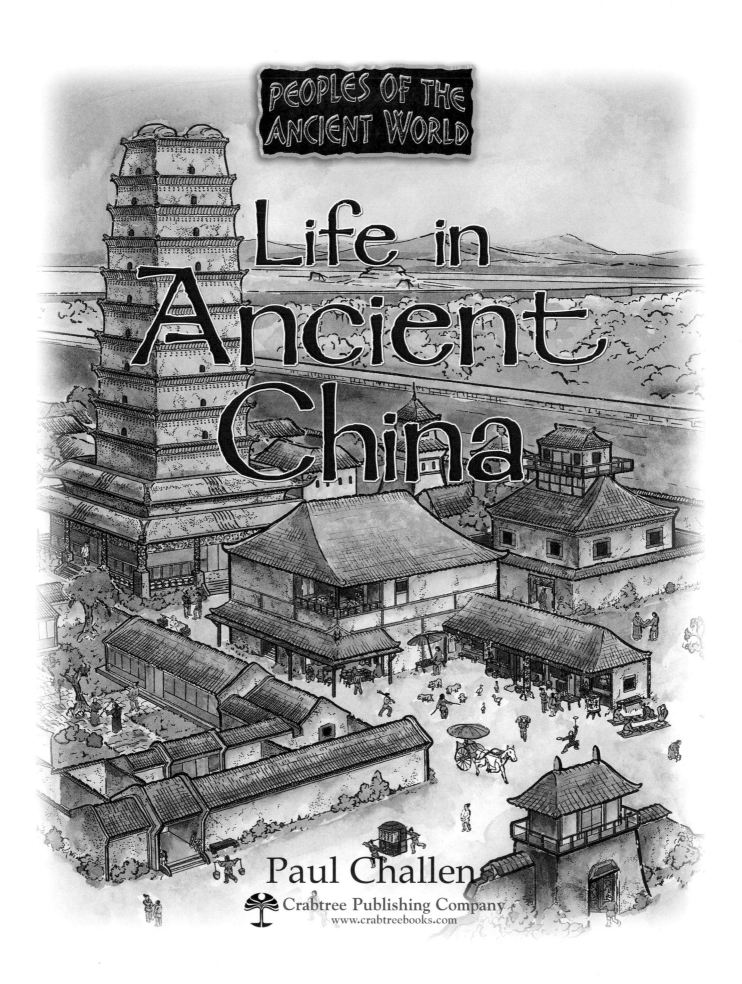

PEOPLES OF THE ANCIENT WORLD

Life in Ancient China

Paul Challen

Crabtree Publishing Company
www.crabtreebooks.com

Crabtree Publishing Company
www.crabtreebooks.com

For Sam, Evelina, and Henry

Coordinating editor: Ellen Rodger
Project editor: Sean Charlebois
Editors: Rachel Eagen, Carrie Gleason, Adrianna Morganelli
Production coordinator: Rosie Gowsell
Production assistance: Samara Parent
Scanning technician: Arlene Arch-Wilson
Photo research: Allison Napier
Art director: Rob MacGregor

Project management assistance:
Media Projects, Inc.
Carter Smith
Pat Smith
Laura Smyth
Aimee Kraus
Michael Greenhut

Consultant: Jeremy Murray, M.A., Columbia University, Department of Asian Studies

Photographs: Asian Art & Archaeology, Inc./CORBIS: p. 25; Bettmann/CORBIS: p. 30; Bildarchiv Preussischer Kulturbesitz / Art Resource, NY: p. 18; Burstein Collection/CORBIS: p. 9; Charles & Josette Lenars/CORBIS: p. 8; China Span, LLC/CORBIS: p. 25; The Cover Story/CORBIS: p. 7 (bottom); Fotosearch: p. 14, p. 23, p. 31; Giraudon/Art Resource, NY: p. 9 (top); Joseph Sohm; ChromoSohm Inc./CORBIS: pp. 4–5; Alfred Ko/CORBIS: p. 13; National Palace Museum, Taiwan: p. 18; Keren Su/CORBIS: p. 7 (top), p. 12 (bottom), p. 16 (top); Snark/Art Resource, NY: p. 15; Sonia Halliday: p. 28, p. 29; Joseph Sohm; ChromoSohm Inc./CORBIS: pp. 30–31; Werner Forman/Art Resource, NY: p. 10, p. 15

Illustrations: James Burmester: p. 24; Roman Goforth p. 17, p. 19, pp. 20–21, Rose Gowsell: borders, p. 5 (dragon), p. 23; Robert MacGregor: pp. 4–5 (timeline), p. 6 (map), p. 13 (map); Ole Skedsmo: p. 1, p. 12, pp. 26–27

Cartography: Jim Chernishenko: p. 13

Cover: Illustration of Buddhist figure Avalokiteshvara, Guide of Souls, from about 900 A.D.

Title page: A Chinese village.

Contents: Emperor Shi Huangdi was buried with thousands of terracotta clay soldiers. The ancient Chinese believed that the clay army would help protect the emperor's spirit in the next world.

Icon: The dragon was a symbol of ancient Chinese legend.

Back Cover: Buddhism was a religion from India that was introduced to ancient China.

Crabtree Publishing Company
www.crabtreebooks.com   1-800-387-7650

Printed in the USA/122009/CG20090903

Cataloging-in-Publication data

Challen, Paul C. (Paul Clarence), 1967-
    Life in ancient China / written by Paul Challen.
        p. cm. -- (Peoples of the ancient world)
    Includes index.
    ISBN 0-7787-2037-3 (rlb) -- ISBN 0-7787-2067-5 (pbk)
        1. China--Civilization--Juvenile literature. I. Title. II. Series.
DS721.C47213 2005
931--dc22

                                        2004013067
                                             LC

**Published in
the United States**
PMB 59051
350 Fifth Avenue,
59th Floor
New York, New York
10118

**Published
in Canada**
616 Welland Ave.,
St. Catharines,
Ontario, Canada
L2M 5V6

**Published in the
United Kingdom**
Maritime House
Basin Road North,
Hove
BN41 1WR

**Published
in Australia**
386 Mt. Alexander Rd.,
Ascot Vale (Melbourne)
V1C 3032

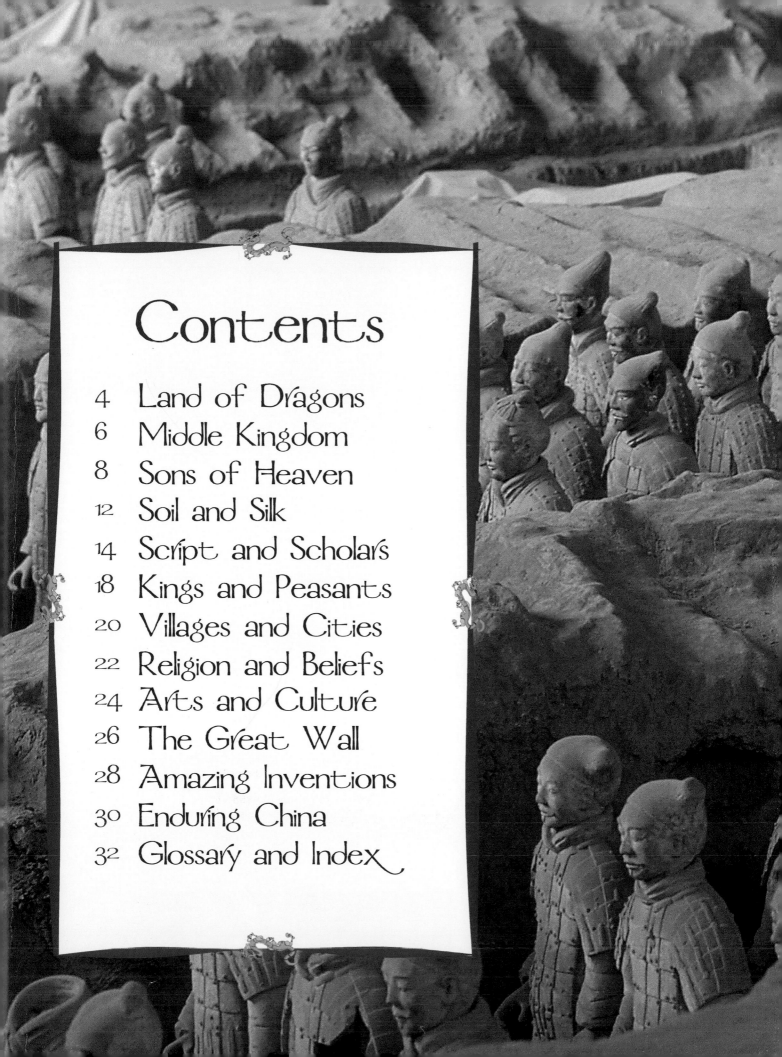

Contents

Land of Dragons

Ancient China was one of the most advanced civilizations the world has ever known. For most of its 7,000-year history, lack of easy land or sea routes stopped travelers from other parts of the world from visiting China. This made China a prosperous **and independent society.**

Life in ancient China was dominated by kings and emperors. A series of rulers from the same family was called a dynasty. Several dynasties governed China's enormous land and its large population of farmers, artisans, scholars, merchants, government officials, and slaves. China grew from a collection of small farming villages into large cities, where markets and culture flourished. The ancient Chinese developed a system of writing so that people all over China could communicate with each other. Numerous inventions such as paper, printing, and a counting machine called the abacus, improved the daily lives of the Chinese people. The inventions also helped spread trade and religious ideas across China. Many of ancient China's advances were adopted by peoples around the world and are used today.

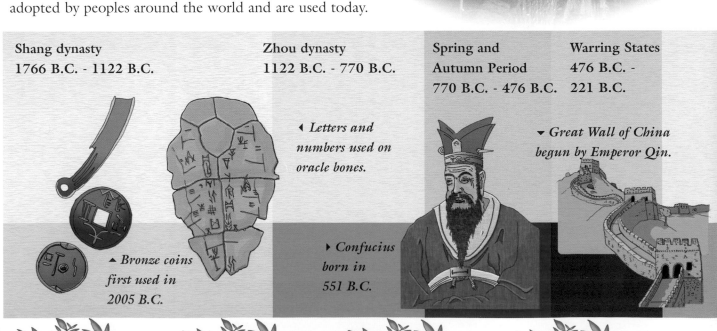

Shang dynasty
1766 B.C. - 1122 B.C.

▲ *Bronze coins first used in 2005 B.C.*

Zhou dynasty
1122 B.C. - 770 B.C.

◄ *Letters and numbers used on oracle bones.*

▶ *Confucius born in 551 B.C.*

Spring and Autumn Period
770 B.C. - 476 B.C.

Warring States
476 B.C. - 221 B.C.

▼ *Great Wall of China begun by Emperor Qin.*

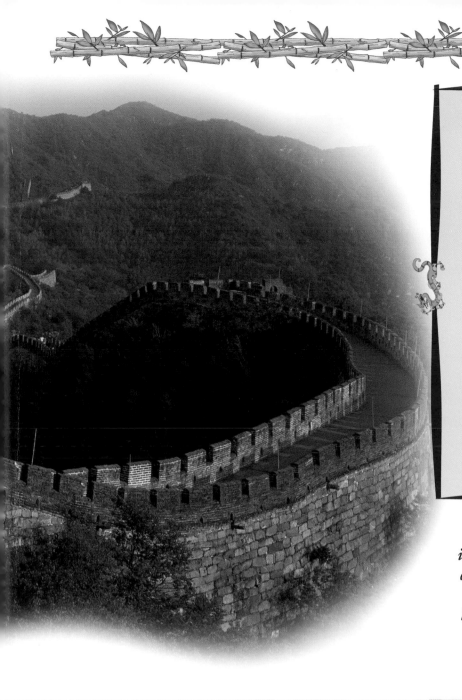

What is a "civilization?"

Most historians agree that a civilization is a group of people that shares common languages, some form of writing, advanced technology and science, and systems of government and religion.

◀ *To protect ancient China from invaders from the north, China's first emperor built a large wooden barrier called the Long Wall. The wall was later rebuilt using bricks and became the Great Wall, which still stretches thousands of miles across China.*

Han dynasty 206 B.C. - 220 A.D.	Jin dynasty 265-420	Wei dynasty 386 - 618	Tang dynasty 618 - 907	Song dynasty 960 - 1280
▼ *New religion of Buddhism spreads through China.*	▼ *Fireworks invented.*		▼ *Empress Wu, China's only female ruler born in 624.*	▼ *Kublai Khan meets European explorer Marco Polo in 1275.*

Middle Kingdom

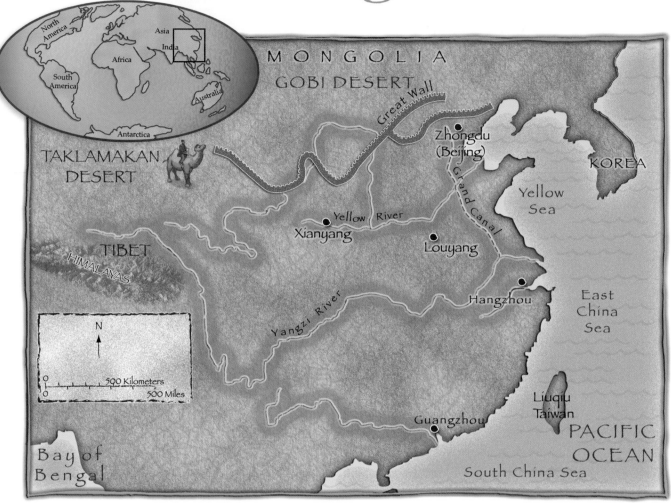

China's geography and natural features were important factors in the growth of its civilization. China stretched across a large section of central and eastern Asia. Tall mountains, large deserts, and vast seas protected the people from invaders. Rivers created fertile farmland where the Chinese people grew crops, and built houses, villages, and cities.

Crucial Rivers

Rivers were a source of life for the early peoples of China. **Silt** that flowed downstream fertilized the land on either side of the rivers and created rich soil that was ideal for farming. By about 5000 B.C., the Yangshao peoples began settling in the northern Yellow River Valley. In the south, where the climate was warmer, settlements began along the Yangzi River. Over time, the Chinese began practicing agriculture and founded permanent villages along these rivers, using the water to **irrigate** crops. The abundance of crops helped village populations grow.

▲ *The Chinese called their land* jung guo, *or the Middle Kingdom. They believed China was the center, or middle, of the universe.*

River of Sorrows

Heavy rains and melting snow in the mountains caused both the Yangzi and the Yellow Rivers to flood nearly every summer, allowing farmers to plant and irrigate extra crops. Sometimes the floods killed people and destroyed crops, leading to **famine**. The Yellow River was nicknamed the "River of Sorrows" because of the death it sometimes caused.

Bamboo

In ancient China, southern forests were filled with bamboo trees. Bamboo was used for food, clothing, housing, and transportation. Books and most musical instruments were also made of bamboo.

▼ *Daily life along the banks of the Yellow River is much the same today as it was thousands of years ago.*

▲ *Traveling through the Taklamakan Desert in western China was very dangerous. "Taklamakan" means "enter and you shall never return."*

Sons of Heaven

The ancient Chinese people called their emperors "Sons of Heaven," because they believed the leaders were chosen by the gods. Emperors had many wives and many children. When an emperor died, his eldest son usually became emperor. Some Chinese dynasties lasted for hundreds of years. Emperors were China's supreme political, military, and religious leaders.

Mandate of Heaven

Emperors were expected to act in the best interest of the Chinese people. The Chinese believed that their **ancestors** in heaven brought prosperity and protection to them when an emperor was fair and just. If an emperor acted badly, or was a poor military leader, the heavenly ancestors were thought to show their displeasure by sending earthquakes, floods, and droughts. The people took the natural disasters as a sign to rebel and replace the emperor. The Chinese people called this the Mandate of Heaven.

Shang and Zhou Dynasties

China's first known dynasties were founded by the Shang and Zhou peoples. The Shang had large armies with horse-drawn **chariots** and gained control of northern China around 1750 B.C. Shang kings set up large cities and ruled for 600 years. The Zhou people came from the western border of the Shang kingdom and conquered the Shang. Through constant warfare, the Zhou made their kingdom larger, and changed the way China was governed. Zhou kings allowed warriors, or nobles, to own land if they promised to fight for the king in war. This made the nobles more powerful and the king weaker.

▲ *Qin Shi Huangdi founded the Qin dynasty and was China's first emperor. The word "China" comes from the name "Qin."*

Han Dynasty

The Han dynasty was founded by a government official named Liu Bang in 206 B.C. Over 400 years, the Han emperors expanded China's boundaries and brought peace and prosperity to the people. The Han dynasty organized a civil service to run the empire. The civil service was run by government officials who collected taxes, made sure laws were followed, and kept roads and canals in good shape. With people across China following the same laws, a common Chinese culture developed. Today, most Chinese think of themselves as **descendants** of the Han.

◀ *After the Han dynasty ended, China's nobles fought each other for power. It took the strong leadership of Emperor Wendi (center) to end the fighting and reunite China.*

Qin Dynasty

In 221 B.C., a ruler named Shi Huangdi came to power. Qin Shi Huangdi moved China's capital to Xianyang and forced nobles to move there with him. By keeping his nobles close to him, Qin Shi Huangdi was able to make sure they did not rebel against him. Qin Shi Huangdi made strict laws and **taxed** everyone in China. Anyone who opposed his laws was brutally punished. He ordered officials who protested against him to be thrown into a pit and buried alive. When Qin Shi Huangdi died, rebellions broke out and the Qin dynasty collapsed.

▶ *Emperors ruled from a palace built in the center of China's capital city. The emperor wore fine silks in the royal color of yellow.*

The Sui Dynasty

The Sui dynasty made many changes that strengthened China. Emperor Wendi brought smaller village leaders under his central control and established a census to count people. He also made punishments for lawbreaking the same in every part of the country. China became wealthy during the Sui dynasty and Emperor Wendi reduced the amount of taxes people had to pay. When Wendi's son became emperor, he raised taxes and forced farmers to work on large construction projects, such as the Grand Canal. This made the emperor unpopular and he was **assassinated**, bringing an end to the Sui dynasty.

◄ *A large army protected every Chinese dynasty. During the Han dynasty, the army was made up of professional soldiers. They wore bronze armor, shields and helmets, high boots, and padded garments. This soldier carries a* qiang, *or spear.*

▼ *The Grand Canal was built during the Sui dynasty to link China's Yellow and Yangzi Rivers. Boats used the canal to carry food and soldiers across the empire. Emperors forced one member from every family to work as laborers on the canal.*

The Tang Dynasty

The Tang dynasty, which began in 618 A.D., marked a period of great advancement in Chinese culture. This period is referred to as China's Golden Age. Great artistic achievements, such as porcelain making, were developed during the Tang dynasty. Porcelain was made by painting a bright blue dye on clay objects that were not yet dry. A clear glaze was then applied to the clay and it was fired in a kiln, or large oven. Chinese artists began decorating porcelain with elaborate paintings that told the history of the Tang dynasty. Using their powerful armies, China expanded north to what is modern-day Korea, south to modern Vietnam, and west to India during the Tang dynasty. The collapse of the Tang dynasty in 906 A.D. brought disorder to China again.

The Song Dynasty

A military leader who became known as Taizu founded the Song dynasty in 960 A.D. Taizu **reformed** the Chinese military and government so that people got jobs based on their skill instead of favoritism. The Song built sea-going ships called junks to take Chinese merchants to foreign lands. As trade increased, Chinese merchants became wealthy. Merchants spent money supporting artists, which made the Song era a great period of Chinese art. In the 1100s, most of the ruling Song family was put in prison when the Jin attacked from the north and established the Jin dynasty. A Song son fled south, where he began the Southern Song dynasty in 1127 A.D. Both the Jin and Southern Song were defeated by invading warriors called the Mongols.

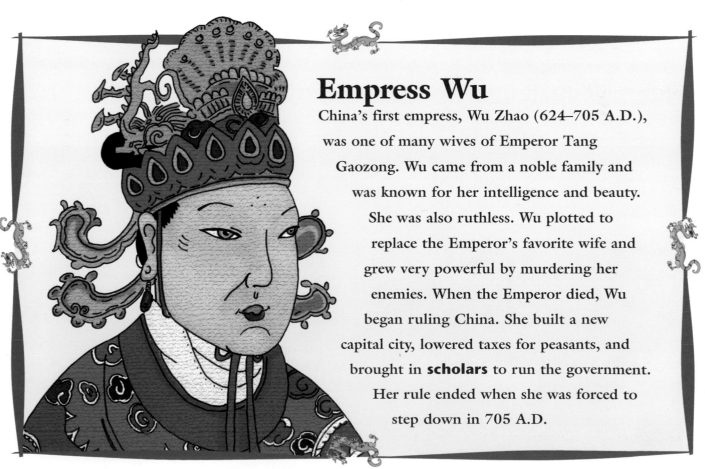

Empress Wu

China's first empress, Wu Zhao (624–705 A.D.), was one of many wives of Emperor Tang Gaozong. Wu came from a noble family and was known for her intelligence and beauty. She was also ruthless. Wu plotted to replace the Emperor's favorite wife and grew very powerful by murdering her enemies. When the Emperor died, Wu began ruling China. She built a new capital city, lowered taxes for peasants, and brought in **scholars** to run the government. Her rule ended when she was forced to step down in 705 A.D.

Soil and Silk

The Chinese people depended on farming and trading. Over many years, China developed a network of routes across Asia to trade its crops and goods. The development of using coins as money made trade easier.

Fertile River Valleys

The Yellow and Yangzi Rivers made China very good for farming. Most years, the rivers flooded and left a rich, fertile topsoil, or silt, on the surrounding land that made planting and growing easy. Chinese farmers also used the rivers to irrigate their fields.

Farming

Most Chinese were peasant farmers who grew crops on small plots of land. All family members were expected to work on these farms, which grew crops such as millet, rice, and wheat for people in the army and in the cities. Farmers used simple wooden or stone tools and most labor was done by hand. Farm animals were not common, so families often used their own waste as **fertilizer**. Painted clay pots were used to store the harvest.

▲ *Chinese farmers used oxen and water buffalo to pull plows made of iron to till the soil.*

▼ *Peasants in southern China planted rice shoots in terraced rice paddy fields when they were flooded.*

THE SILK ROAD

▲ *The Chinese built a network of roads and canals to allow people to trade with each other. The most famous trade route was the Silk Road, which stretched from China across Asia to the Mediterranean Sea. Along the Silk Road, merchants traveled by camel across deserts to trade Chinese silk, tea, and spices for gold, silver, and precious stones from Central Asia.*

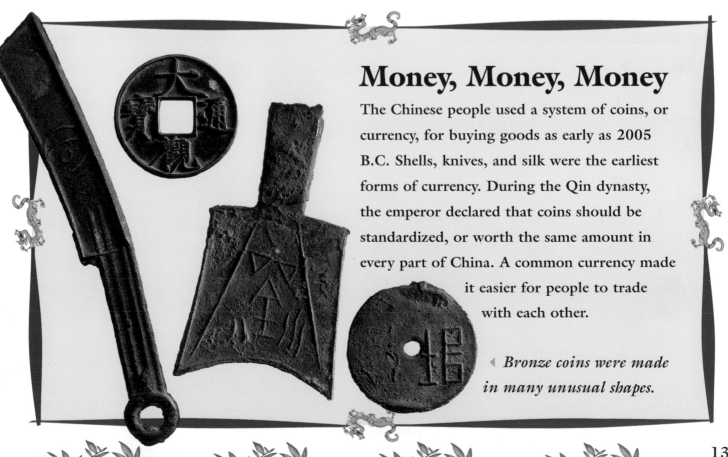

Money, Money, Money

The Chinese people used a system of coins, or currency, for buying goods as early as 2005 B.C. Shells, knives, and silk were the earliest forms of currency. During the Qin dynasty, the emperor declared that coins should be standardized, or worth the same amount in every part of China. A common currency made it easier for people to trade with each other.

◀ *Bronze coins were made in many unusual shapes.*

Script and Scholars

The ancient Chinese developed their own language and systems of writing and record-keeping. Technical advances, such as the development of inks and paper, allowed the ancient Chinese to record history, keep track of time, and add and subtract numbers.

Spoken Language

Over hundreds of years, the spoken Chinese language went through several changes. During the Zhou dynasty, Old, or Archaic, Chinese was spoken. Not much is known about what Old Chinese sounded like. During the time of the Sui, Tang, and Song dynasties, a new form of the Chinese language, known as Middle Chinese, was used. By 1000 A.D., a number of different dialects, or versions, had emerged, many of which survive today.

▶ *Before paper was available, bamboo was used to write on. Chinese characters were cut into thin strips of bamboo beginning at the top.*

Writing Without An Alphabet

China does not have an alphabet that combines letters to form words like other languages. Chinese writing uses characters, or symbols, to represent words and ideas. There are about 40,000 Chinese characters and each one can be made up of as many as 26 brushstrokes. To read a Chinese newspaper, a person might need to know about 3,000 of these characters. Most Chinese characters have changed very little since the Qin dynasty, when the emperor ordered that writing be standardized.

	to fish	horse
1700 B.C.-1400 B.C.		
776 B.C.-250 B.C.		
250 B.C.-25 A.D.		
25 A.D.-200 A.D.		
380 A.D.-Present	漁	馬

Writing Systems

Writing was first used in China for religious ceremonies. In 1400 B.C., Shang religious leaders, or priests, carved questions to the gods on sheep bones and turtle shells. These bones became known as oracle bones. By about 400 B.C., artisans began writing on bamboo strips, wooden tablets, and coated silk cloth using ink made from soot or charcoal mixed with water and glue. Writing usually described great historical events, such as military battles or the rise of an emperor. Government officials during the Qin dynasty introduced a standardized form of writing across China to ensure that educated people understood the emperor's commands.

▲ *Most people in ancient China did not know how to write. Educated men studied to become scribes. Scribes copied important papers and books for the emperor.*

◀ *Shang priests put questions on oracle bones and then looked for answers in the cracks made when the bones were heated.*

Ancient Calculators

The ancient Chinese called mathematics *suan chu*, or "the art of calculation." Number symbols found on oracle bones from the Shang dynasty date back 3,400 years. Chinese numbers are based on the decimal system, or the number ten, just as most number systems are today. The ancient Chinese used mathematics for many purposes, such as building construction, flood control, and to calculate sums for trading goods.

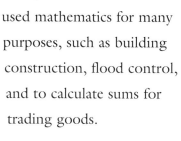

◄ *The Chinese invented the abacus, a counting tool that used rods and sliding beads. The abacus is still used in some parts of China.*

The Chinese Calendar

Mathematics was used to develop the Chinese calendar. The ancient Chinese divided each year into twelve months. Unlike other calendars that are based on the cycles of the sun, the Chinese calendar is based on the cycles of the moon. One full **lunar phase** of 28 days represents a month. The cycles of the moon are different from the cycles of the sun, so Chinese New Year happens each year between late January and early February instead of on January 1.

▲ *The signs used for the numbers one through nine during the Shang dynasty are shown above.*

▲ *(top) The art of Tai Chi may be based on the natural world. Some people believe Tai Chi was developed by a priest who copied the movements of a white crane preying on a snake. Once used for fighting, Tai Chi evolved into a gentle form of exercise practiced by people of all ages.*

Public Education

Education became very important during the Han dynasty. Around 100 B.C., Emperor Wudi agreed with the great Chinese thinker Confucius, that the key to good government depended on education. Wudi started a system of public schools for boys in every part of China that taught the ideas of Confucius. In the capital of China, there was a major school called the Grand School. The Grand School started out with only 50 students but within 100 years it had more than 30,000 students!

The Chinese Zodiac

The ancient Chinese developed a system for keeping track of the years using twelve different animals. According to a legend, the **zodiac** originated with **Buddhism**. The Buddha called all the animals of China to his bedside but only twelve came. To honor the animals for coming, he created a year for each one. Each animal has its own characteristics. Some Chinese believe that people born in a certain year will have the characteristics of that year's animal. A person born in the year 1995, was born in the Chinese Year of the Pig, and would be caring and determined.

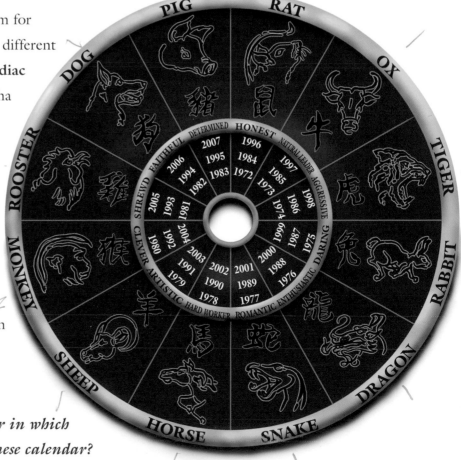

▸ *Can you find the name of the year in which you were born according to the Chinese calendar?*

Kings and Peasants

China's people were divided into groups, called social classes, based on birth, wealth, and the kind of work they did. These social classes were the basis of Chinese society. Everything from where people lived to what they ate and wore, depended on their social class.

Cooking Classes

In northern China, boiled noodles, soybeans, and baked breads were common foods. In the south, where farmers planted large rice fields, boiled rice was the main dish, and fresh fruit and seafood were also common. In the western mountains, people flavored their food with hot peppers and other spices. Wealthier Chinese often ate meats such as pork, lamb, duck, and pigeon, and for special feasts, snakes, dogs, or bear claws. Most Chinese ate two meals a day. The first meal was at mid-morning and the other came before nightfall. The most important item in the Chinese kitchen was the stove, which burned wood to heat the food.

Dress Codes

The clothing, hats, and jewelry worn by a Chinese person showed what position that person had in society. Wealthy people usually wore expensive silk, while peasants wore long shirt-like clothing made of hemp, a fabric woven from plant fiber. Men almost always wore hats when they went out in public.

▲ *Noblewomen usually wore their long hair in topknots that were held together with hairpins.*

◄ *This pottery figure dates back to the Tang dynasty. It shows the types of clothing wealthy government officials wore.*

18

Royal Palace

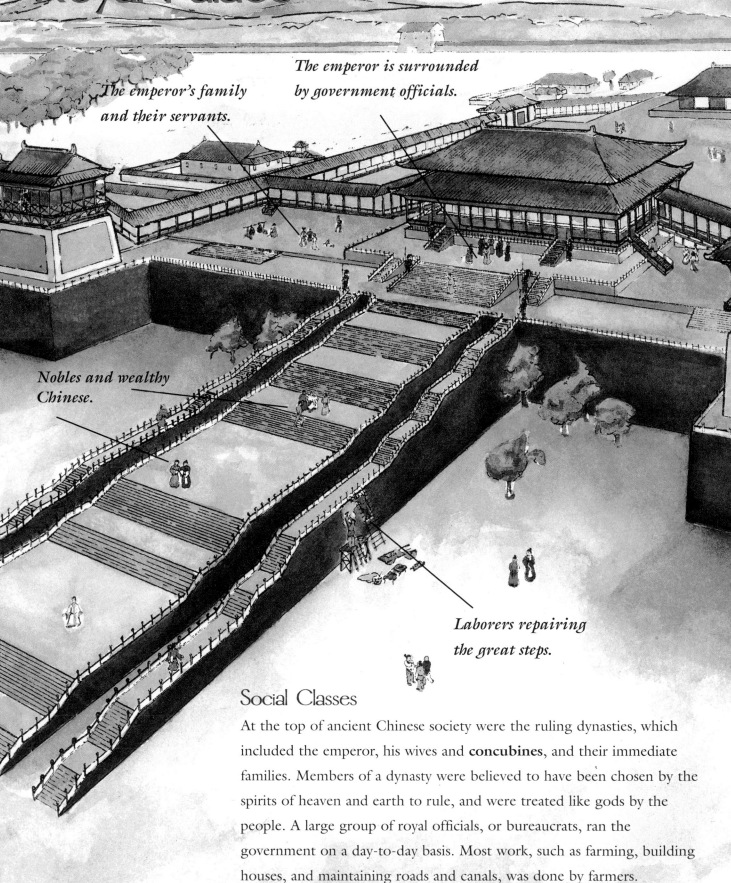

The emperor's family and their servants.

The emperor is surrounded by government officials.

Nobles and wealthy Chinese.

Laborers repairing the great steps.

Social Classes

At the top of ancient Chinese society were the ruling dynasties, which included the emperor, his wives and **concubines**, and their immediate families. Members of a dynasty were believed to have been chosen by the spirits of heaven and earth to rule, and were treated like gods by the people. A large group of royal officials, or bureaucrats, ran the government on a day-to-day basis. Most work, such as farming, building houses, and maintaining roads and canals, was done by farmers.

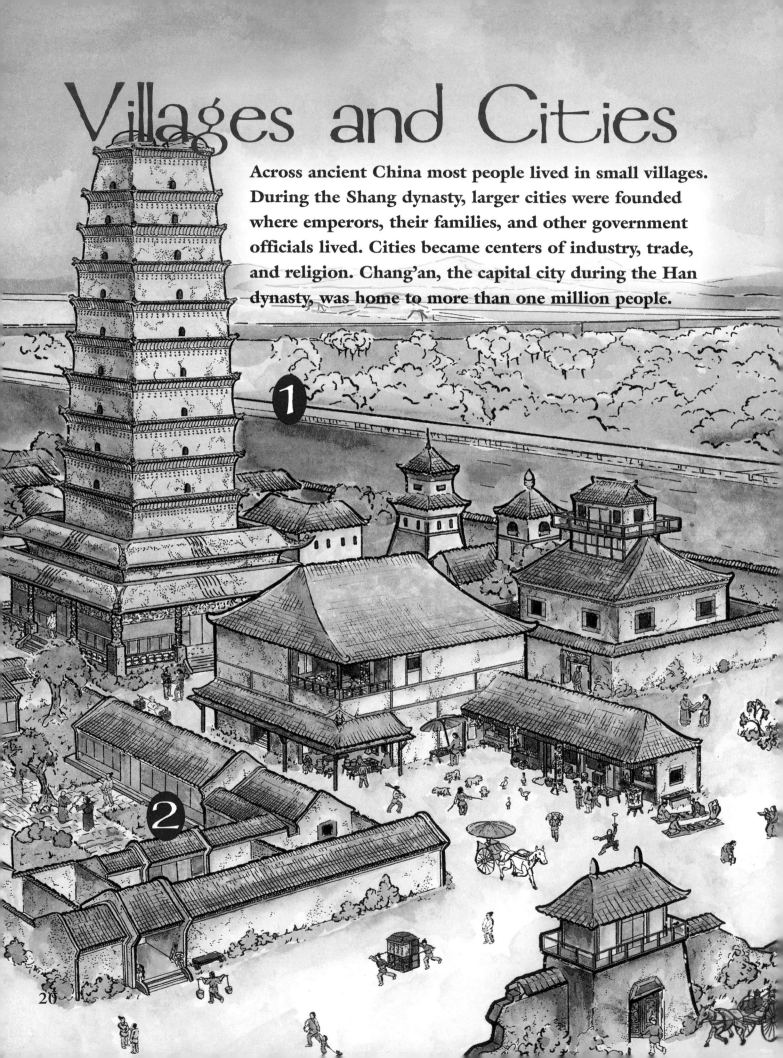

Villages and Cities

Across ancient China most people lived in small villages. During the Shang dynasty, larger cities were founded where emperors, their families, and other government officials lived. Cities became centers of industry, trade, and religion. Chang'an, the capital city during the Han dynasty, was home to more than one million people.

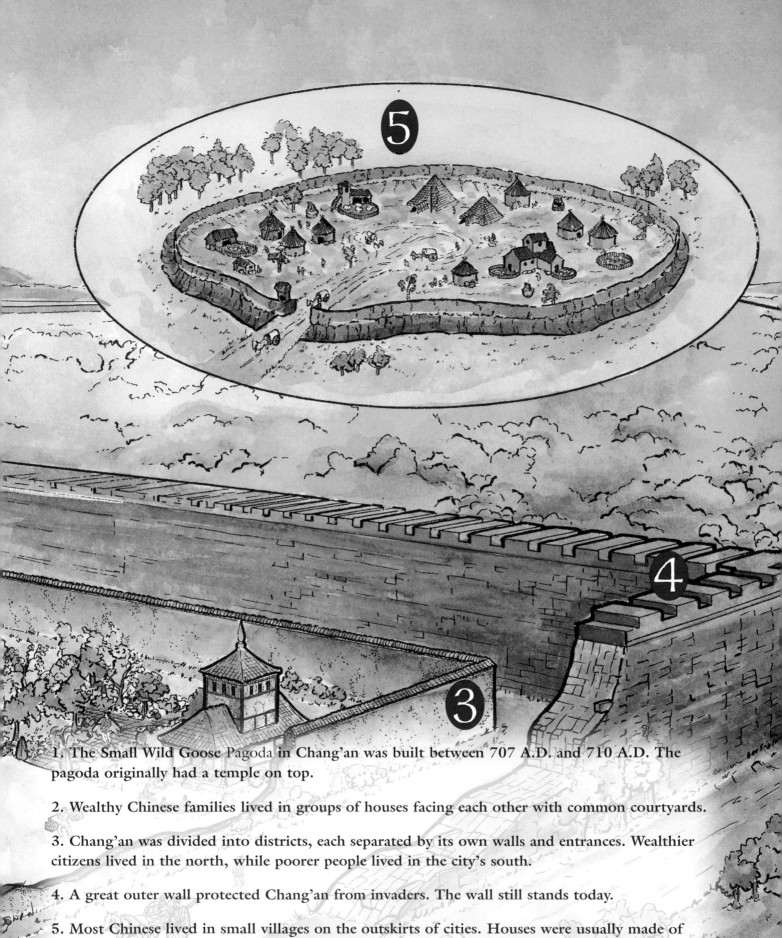

1. The Small Wild Goose Pagoda in Chang'an was built between 707 A.D. and 710 A.D. The pagoda originally had a temple on top.

2. Wealthy Chinese families lived in groups of houses facing each other with common courtyards.

3. Chang'an was divided into districts, each separated by its own walls and entrances. Wealthier citizens lived in the north, while poorer people lived in the city's south.

4. A great outer wall protected Chang'an from invaders. The wall still stands today.

5. Most Chinese lived in small villages on the outskirts of cities. Houses were usually made of wood covered with a plaster of mud. Villages had central meeting places, and areas such as underground pits where grain and other food was stored.

Religion and Beliefs

Ancient Chinese religion and philosophy **were based around four different belief systems, or ways of thinking. These were ancestor worship, Taoism, Confucianism, and Buddhism. Most ancient Chinese followed ideas contained in one of these systems.**

Ancestor Worship

Family was at the center of ancient Chinese society. Family included all current relatives, ancestors from the past, as well as from future generations. Respect for past generations was so important that many people prayed to the spirits of their ancestors for help and guidance. In most ancient Chinese homes there was an **altar** where offerings could be made to dead relatives. The family name was very important to the ancient Chinese. The family name was carried on only through the male members of the family, so people felt it was important to have sons as heirs.

▶ *Confucius was known as The Master. His teachings are in a book called The Analects.*

Confucianism

Confucius was a scholar who lived from 551 B.C. to 479 B.C. Confucius was born into a wealthy family, but war caused his family to become poor. To improve himself, Confucius began to study. He became one of the wisest men in China. Confucius developed a system of rules of behavior. The rules stated that sons owed loyalty to fathers, wives owed loyalty to husbands, and younger brothers owed loyalty to older brothers. Confucius believed that if these rules were followed, Chinese society would be more peaceful. Just as a father was responsible for caring for his family, Confucius believed the emperor was responsible for treating his subjects wisely and fairly. Confucius thought children should obey their elders and the Chinese people should obey their emperor.

▲ *Many Buddhist temples were built as places of prayer.*

Buddhism

Buddhism is based on the teachings of Siddhartha Gautama, who
became known as the Buddha, or "Enlightened One." Gautama
became saddened by the suffering in the world and decided to go on
a journey from his home in India. Gautama felt that he had found the
meaning of life after **meditating** near a tree. Followers of Buddha, called
Buddhists, believe that people suffer because they want things and they will
only be happy once they stop wanting things. Buddhism spread through China
between 1 A.D. and 100 A.D.

▲ *The Buddha
taught that people
could be born again,
or reincarnated,
many times.*

Taoism

Between 600 and 500 B.C., a way of thinking known as Taoism developed
in China. Taoism is based on the *Tao Te Ching*, a book written by a teacher
named Lao Tzu. Lao Tzu taught the importance of harmony
with nature and that achieving a balance of the forces of
yin and *yang* is the key to spiritual peace. Lao Tzu
created Taoism to end the constant fighting in
Chinese society. Tzu believed fighting was a sign that
yin and y*ang* were out of balance. In 440 A.D., the
emperor declared Taoism a national religion. From
then on, Lao Tzu was honored as a god.

◀ *The Tao operates
by balancing* yin
and yang, *the
opposing forces
in the universe.*

Arts and Culture

Every educated person in ancient China was expected to practice the four arts of music, calligraphy, chess, and brush painting. The ancient Chinese love of the arts spread to include works created by professional artists, musicians, and scribes employed by the emperor.

Music

Ancient Chinese music, or *qin*, was played at banquets, ceremonies, and in the court of the emperor and other nobles. Musical instruments, such as the Chinese flute, or *xiao*, date back 9,000 years. The Chinese lute, or *pipa*, was sometimes played by noblewomen at court. During solemn occasions, such as funerals, musicians played bells.

Calligraphy

Calligraphy, or *shu*, is the Chinese art of depicting written characters on paper. Poets were often **calligraphers**, who illustrated their poems using the fancy writing. Calligraphers used brushes made from animal hair tied with silk, and fastened into bamboo tubes. Ink was made by rubbing drops of water on a solid inkstone, formed from burned pine soot and gum. It took many years to learn the art of calligraphy.

Chinese Chess

Chinese chess was called *qi*. It is based on a game from India called Chanturanga, which may have been brought to China by Buddhist **missionaries**. The game board is set up to represent two enemy countries that are separated by a river. Players move pieces along the lines on the board in an attempt to capture their opponent's King.

▲ *Calligraphy conveys a word's meaning attractively. The word above is "harmony."*

◄ *A musician plays the guqin, a Chinese zither with 25 strings.*

Brush Painting

The Chinese art of brush painting, or *hua*, dates back at least 6,000 years. Painting was originally done to decorate pottery or bronze statues. After Buddhism arrived in China, painting took on a religious role. Painted religious murals were found in carved grottoes, or caves, as well as in Buddhist temples. By 300 A.D., artists began painting beautiful landscape paintings that were not **realistic**, but expressed the artist's emotions using soft colors. By the time of the Song Dynasty (960 to 1280 A.D.), people and stories from everyday life had become popular subjects for paintings.

▼ *Jade stone was carved with bronze-tipped drills. Wood and leather polishing wheels were used to make it shine.*

Artisans

Many artisans in ancient China created works of art from bronze, jade, and clay. Bronze was made by combining copper and tin. Metal workers poured molten, or hot liquid, bronze into ceramic molds. When the bronze cooled, the mold was broken to reveal works of art, such as statues, vases, and drinking vessels. The Chinese also used a form of baked clay called terracotta to fashion sculptures and figures.

Kung Fu

Another art that came to China after Buddhism arrived, is the martial, or military, art known as Kung Fu. Kung Fu is based on the idea that physical health consists of both inner and outer strength. While physical exercises kept the outer body strong, breathing exercises were meant to help give fuel to the body's inner organs. By the 1200s, Kung Fu had spread across Asia. As Chinese Kung Fu spread, it developed into Karate in Japan, and into Taekwando in Korea.

The Great Wall

Ancient China's greatest legacy is the Great Wall. This huge wall, which measures 2,150 miles (3,460 km), was built by Qin Shi Huangdi to protect his kingdom from tribes to the north who threatened to invade China.

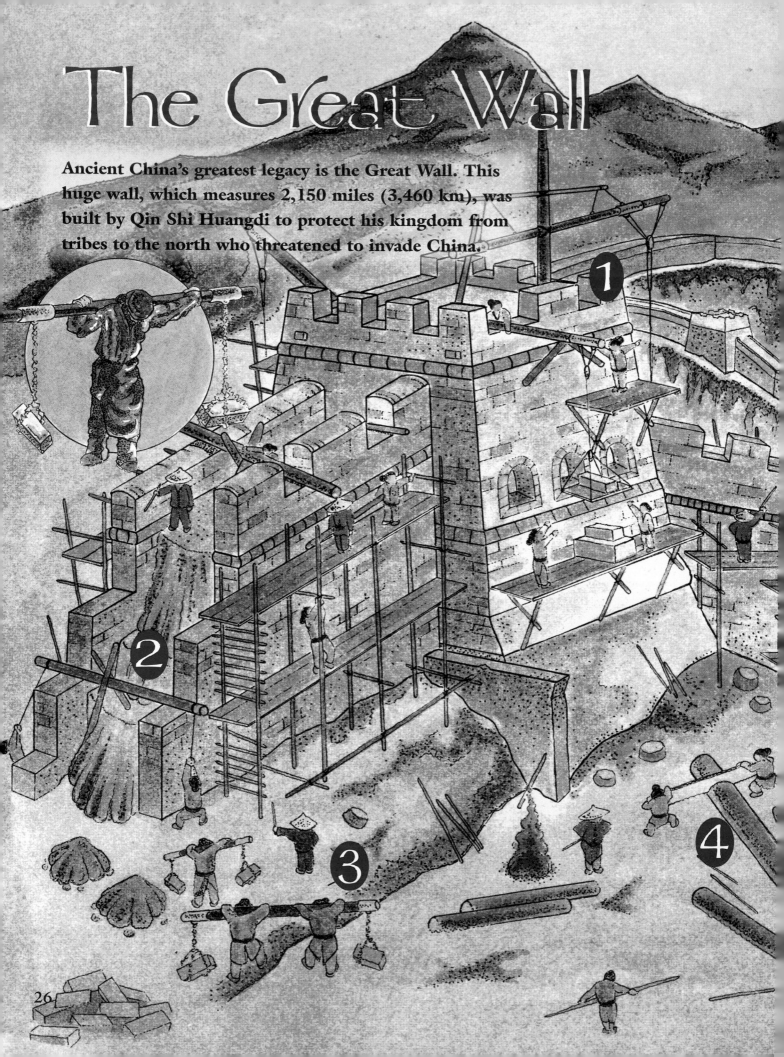

1. The Great Wall was built with many towers where Chinese soldiers took up posts to watch for invaders. Soldiers signalled from tower to tower using flags, fires, and drums.

2. The inside of the Great Wall is made of soil and rubble. The earliest wall was made of wood, but during the Ming dynasty, the walls were covered with bricks and a road paved on top.

3. Most of the difficult work in building the Great Wall was done by peasant farmers and captured criminals. Workers who died during construction were buried inside the wall.

4. The Great Wall was built using materials that were found nearby, including stones from the mountains, timber from the forests, and earth, sand, and pebbles from the desert.

5. The Great Wall was built by joining together a series of earlier smaller walls. Today, the Great Wall of China is the largest human-made structure in the world.

Amazing Inventions

The ancient Chinese were great inventors. They invented tools that improved their lives, medical procedures to improve their health, and weapons for war.

Paper

The invention of paper made it possible to record China's history. The ancient Chinese made paper by dipping a bamboo screen into a mix of crushed, or pulped, tree bark, rags, and plant pieces. As a thin layer of pulp dried on the screen, it hardened into a sheet of paper. According to legend, paper was first presented to the emperor in 105 A.D. by a government official named Cai Lun, but it is believed that paper was used in China at least 200 years earlier. Wealthier Chinese used paper for writing. The Chinese also used paper to make inventions such as raincoats, umbrellas, and children's kites.

Printing

Printing requires paper, ink, and a surface carved with letters or other symbols. Chinese monks developed a method of printing using marble pillars. They applied wet paper to carved sections of the pillars, which were coated in ink. The words carved on the pillars transferred to the paper. By about 1000 A.D., an inventor named Pi Sheng had created a system of moveable type that used blocks of clay to represent each of the 40,000 Chinese characters.

▲ *The Chinese made paper out of strips of silk and bamboo. Pulp for paper was later made from bark, hemp, and worn-out nets.*

Gunpowder

The Chinese invented gunpowder by mistake. Chemists were mixing two **chemical** compounds, sulphur and nitrate, to make a potion that would allow the emperor to live forever. Instead, it caused explosions. By the time of the Tang dynasty, the Chinese were using gunpowder, which they called *huoyao*, in war.

▲ *The Chinese used gunpowder to make fireworks. Fireworks were first used in fire rockets, which were ignited in battle to confuse enemies.*

Chinese Medicine

Ancient Chinese medicine was closely tied to Taoism and was concerned with keeping people healthy instead of curing illness. The Chinese believed that a person became sick when *yin* and *yang* were out of balance. Chinese doctors worked to keep *yin* and *yang* in balance by using **herbal** cures and treatments such as acupuncture. To perform acupuncture, ancient Chinese doctors applied small needles to certain spots on the body, called meridans, where they believed life-giving energy flowed. The acupuncture needles eased pain caused by certain illnesses.

Other Inventions

The ancient Chinese also invented the magnetic compass to tell which direction is north. The wheelbarrow was invented to help with construction. The stirrup was invented to make horseback riding easier. All of these inventions continue to be used around the world.

Making Silk

Silk was a rare and valued fabric that ancient Chinese traded with other peoples. Large-scale silk production began as early as the Zhou dynasty. To make silk, the Chinese fed mulberry leaves to caterpillars. When the caterpillars wove cocoons, silk makers boiled the cocoons to loosen the fibers. Then they reeled in the fiber to produce silk, as shown in the illustration.

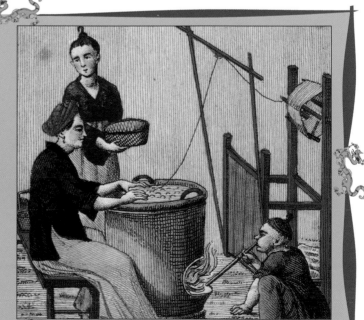

Enduring China

In 1206, people from the north called the Mongols became the first foreign rulers of China. Later, when the Manchu invaded, China's traditions continued to survive. Today, almost 100 years after the rule of the last emperor, Chinese civilization continues to influence the world.

The Mongol Invasion

The area north of China, known as Mongolia, was controlled by the Mongol people. In 1206, a great ruler named Genghis Khan united all Mongol peoples across Asia and captured northern China. His grandson, Kublai Khan, became the emperor of China in 1260. By 1279, he had conquered southern China and founded the Yuan dynasty. The Mongols did not trust the educated members of Chinese society, and did not believe in the teachings of Confucius. The Mongols ended the exam system, which generations of noble Chinese had passed to become government officials.

▸ *Genghis Khan, the fierce leader of the Mongols.*

▾ *Yuan, Ming, and Qing dynasty emperors ruled from Beijing's Forbidden City, which still stands in Tiananmen Square. Common people were not allowed into the Forbidden City.*

Contact with Europeans

The Mongols opened China to greater trade with the rest of the world. In 1275, an Italian explorer named Marco Polo visited Kublai Khan. Marco Polo was amazed by the beautiful artwork and crafts made by Chinese artisans and by China's many scientific and cultural advances. He carried word of China's civilization back to Europe. Many Chinese resented the Mongol rulers. After about 90 years of Yuan dynasty rule, a Buddhist named Ming T'ai Tsu organized an army that forced the Mongols from China. Ming T'ai Tsu then took the throne as the first ruler of the Ming dynasty.

◀ *Puyi, the last emperor of China, was a young boy when he came to power.*

Exploration

During the Ming dynasty, Chinese ships sailed the oceans to explore lands far beyond their shores. In the 1400s, a fleet of huge Chinese ships visited Southeast Asia, India, Arabia, and East Africa. Chinese explorers were not interested in founding **colonies**, so little is known about their journeys.

Modern China

In 1644, the Manchu, another people from the north, invaded China. The Manchu began the Qing dynasty, which lasted until 1912. The Manchu demanded loyalty. Books criticizing the dynasty were destroyed, and many Chinese were forced to shave their heads and wear a single long braid to show obedience to the emperor. The Manchu closed off trade with other countries and banned foreign ships from China's harbors. These actions weakened China's economy. By 1908, the last emperor, Puyi, came to the throne as just a young boy. Four years later, the Chinese leader Sun Yatsen declared China a **republic**, and Puyi gave up the throne. Today, China is a **communist** country.

Glossary

altar A platform used in religious ceremonies

ancestor A person from whom one is descended

assassinate To murder for political reasons

Buddhism A religion founded by Buddha, an ancient religious leader from India

calligrapher An artist who practices the art of producing beautiful handwriting

chariot A two-wheeled cart pulled by horses

chemical A substance with a specific makeup that can be mixed with others to produce a desired effect

colony Distant territories belonging to or under the control of another nation

communist A person who believes in a system of government in which factories, farms, and other property are owned by everyone in common

concubine A mistress or secondary wife

descendant A person who can trace his or her family roots to a certain family group

famine A great shortage of food that causes widespread hunger and starvation

fertilizer A substance, such as manure, that is used in soil to help crops grow faster and larger

herbal Made of plants whose parts are used as a medicine

invaded Entered by force by an enemy

irrigate To supply land with water through ditches, channels, and canals

lunar phase A time period, such as a full moon, during the moon's monthly revolution around the Earth

meditate The act of thinking quietly

missionary A person sent to another land to introduce a religion to others

pagoda A Buddhist religious building

philosophy A set of beliefs about life and the world

prosperous Enjoying wealth and success

realistic Closely resembling real life or nature

reform To make better or improve

republic A government in which power is held by the people, who choose their leaders

scholar A learned person

silt Soil that is carried by water that settles on the bottom of rivers or lakes

tax Money collected from the people by a government

terrace A raised bank of earth with sloping sides used for farming

zodiac An imaginary circle in the sky that is divided into twelve equal parts, each named after a different animal

Index